# CHICAGO

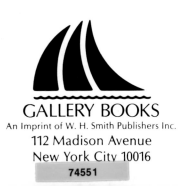

## GALLERY BOOKS
An Imprint of W. H. Smith Publishers Inc.
112 Madison Avenue
New York City 10016

This edition first published in U.S.
in 1990 by Gallery Books,
an imprint of W.H. Smith Publishers, Inc.
112 Madison Avenue, New York, New York 10016


ISBN 0-8317-8831-3


Printed and bound in Spain


For rights information about the photographs in
this book please contact:


The Image Bank
111 Fifth Avenue, New York, NY 10003


Producer: Solomon M. Skolnick
Author: Nancy Millichap Davies
Design Concept: Lesley Ehlers
Designer: Ann-Louise Lipman
Editor: Joan E. Ratajack
Production: Valerie Zars
Photo Researcher: Edward Douglas
Assistant Photo Researcher: Robert V. Hale
Editorial Assistant: Carol Raguso

Title page: *Crossroads of the continent,
Chicago's O'Hare Airport is the busiest
in the U.S., with upwards of 60
million arrivals and departures each
year.* Opposite: *The Sears Tower
(1974), at 1,454 feet the world's tallest
building, dominates the evening
skyline in the city where skyscrapers
were invented.*

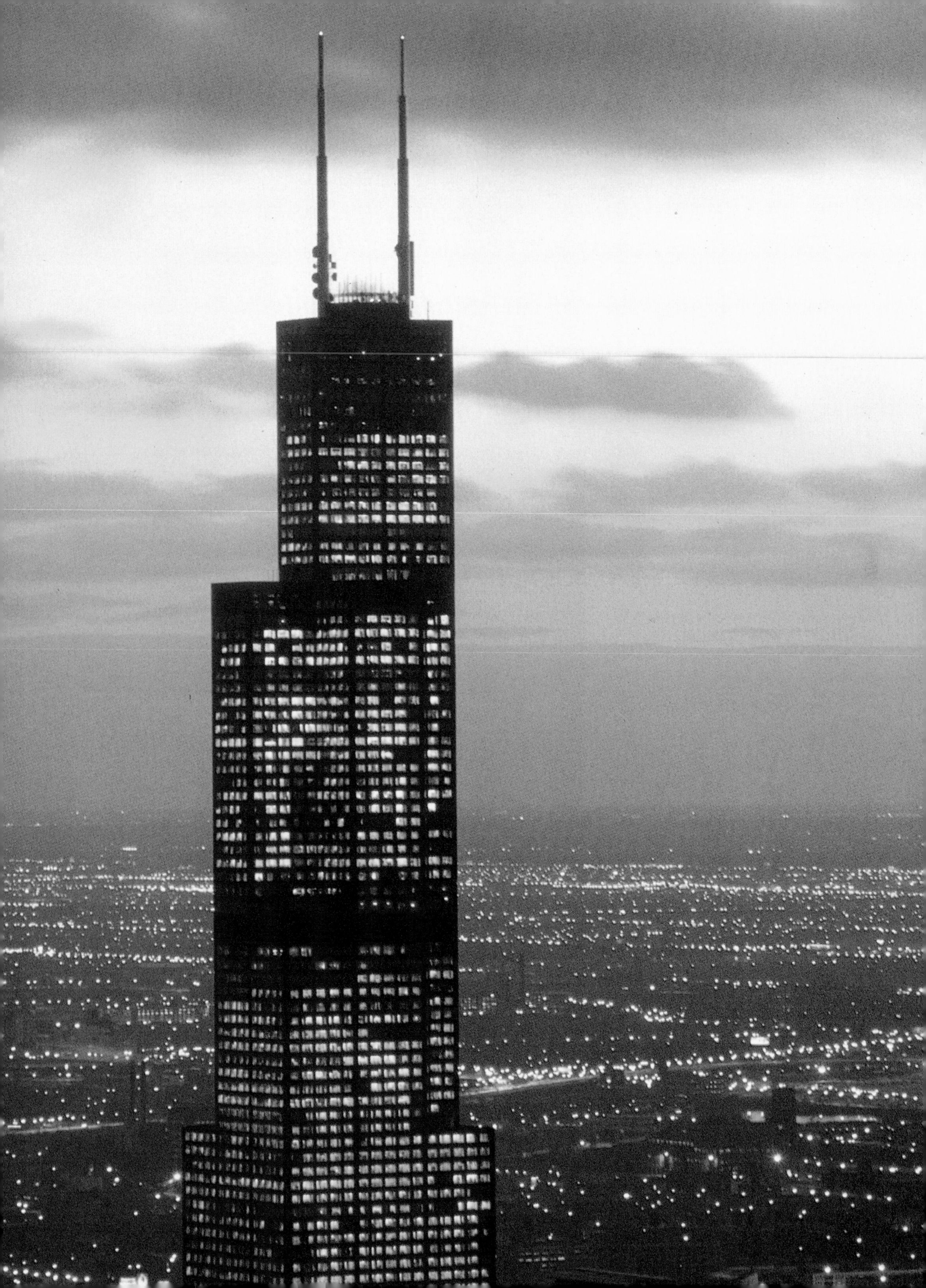

Circling above O'Hare Airport, Chicago's visitors see spread below them the largest urban area between the coasts of the United States. Just over a century and a half ago, it was the frontier. In the era when the great inland city began its development, the colonial period was already history—East coast history at that—and horizons seemed limitless. In the heartland of the young nation, people were determined to find their own solutions rather than look to Europe for answers. Life in a city that sprouted up almost overnight and virtually without a past has made Chicagoans apostles of the new, fascinated with the future and determined to develop fresh answers to the challenges of urban life. Features of the contemporary cityscape which we take for granted—the commercial area with its cluster of gleaming high-rises, the concentrated cultural center in a downtown park, even the very concept of long-range urban planning—were seen as radical departures from the norm in the days when Chicagoans invented them.

Chicago's earliest days gave little hint of the distinctions to come. It was incorporated in 1833 as a town of less than 200 residents in a lakeside marsh of no particular scenic interest. The site had little history of European presence beyond a previous existence as Fort Dearborn, abandoned in 1812 after a massacre of its settlers.

*Beyond the glitter of lakefront high-rises, streetlights chart the way west over the flat expanse of the onetime prairie.*

The word "Chicago" is a variation of the name native Americans of the Miami nation gave the area's river. The name, which meant "strong" or "powerful," may have been an omen. However, since the stream was in fact a sluggish one, the word probably referred to the intensity of the wild garlic which grew at the point where the Chicago River empties into Lake Michigan.

Still, success was not long in coming, at least as measured by population growth. By 1840 the town had nearly 5,000 residents, by 1860 nearly 100,000. In 1890, a million people called Chicago home. In little more than 50 years, the unremarkable town on soggy ground had become a major presence on the national scene.

Chicago's strategic location on the world's largest inland waterway system, the Great Lakes, explains the city's remarkable growth and its economic muscle. Lying at the southern end of Lake Michigan, at the meeting point of water and land routes into the center of the continent, it quickly became the marketing and transportation hub for the rich farmland west and south. In 1916, when Illinois poet Carl Sandburg wrote his

Preceding page: *Distinctive skyline shapes against blue lake waters include the dark, tapered Hancock Building and the twin cylinders of Marina City.* This page, top to bottom: *Landfill operations in the early 1900's created a larger lakefront area for beaches and parks. Polished 1920's elegance marks the hotels and apartment buildings along Lake Shore Drive, once the boundary of Lake Michigan. A lighthouse stands at the eastern tip of the curving spit of sand pumped into the lake in the 1930's to create the North Avenue Beach in Lincoln Park.*

Below: *In July, Chicagoans beat the heat on the city's lakeside beaches.*
Opposite: *Lake Michigan is ice-covered on a minus 30 degree January day.*
Following page: *The 75-foot-square tubes that make up the Sears Tower stand out clearly while the step-like glass front of One South Wacker Drive rises to the left.*

Preceding page: *The 110-story Sears Tower commands sunset skies like a giant sentinel.* This page: *Two of the four identical Presidential Towers bracket the Sears Tower. Below: Alexander Calder's* Universe *graces the Sears lobby. The motor-driven sculpture represents the "big bang" with which the universe theoretically began. Opposite: Commuters speed home by ferry and auto past 333 West Wacker Drive.*

hymn of rough homage "Chicago," he was giving literary form to the city's role as a processing and marketing center for livestock and produce, a role which the city continued to play through the middle of this century. While truck transportation has dispersed the processing of farm products, Chicago remains the center of trade in commodities futures. At the Chicago Board of Trade and the Mercantile Exchange, the two largest such markets in the world, "city slickers," in a deafening din and with elaborate hand signals, sell wheat yet to be harvested and livestock not yet reared.

The lake that proved so important to Chicago's rise is a focal point of the urban scene today. Like "The Hawk," a nickname for the fierce wind that sweeps off the prairies and blows down the straight streets with never a hill to break its force, the lake is an element of nature that shapes Chicago's urban life. Unlike the wind, however, Lake Michigan—or at least its shoreline—has been modified by human effort. The process of extending the lakefront area with landfill began in the 1850's and continued for more than 100 years. Railroads, and later highways, claimed some of the new land which emerged from the lake east of the Loop, the central business district. Instead of using the rest

*The slim profile of 333 West Wacker, snugly fitted to its narrow triangular site, contrasts with the vast bulk of the Merchandise Mart across the river. Following pages: Drawbridges crisscross the Chicago River near the towers of Marina City. Apartments in the complex have pie-shaped rooms. Art deco detailing streamlines the Merchandise Mart (1930), for a time the biggest building anywhere.*

ROBERT MORRIS GEORGE WASHINGTON

for further commercial development, Chicagoans preserved it for a concentration of cultural riches yet to come.

Along today's Lake Michigan shore, parks form an eight-mile-long green ribbon, dotted with cultural institutions and monuments. Behind the parks rise landmark buildings with unobstructed views over the water. The grandest of the public areas, Grant Park, lies just east of the Loop. Within its mile-long expanse, such cultural icons as the Art Institute, the Buckingham Fountain, the Field Museum of Natural History, and the Adler Planetarium stand amid beautiful landscaping. Farther north, Lincoln Park offers a zoo, a conservatory, and even a casting pond. 19 public beaches are available along the lake for residents and visitors alike.

Farsighted lakefront development was one facet of the visionary yet practical Plan of Chicago developed by the architect Daniel Burnham and others in 1909. The first urban plan of its kind devised in the United States, one that built upon a city already in existence and allowed for future expansion, it has strongly influenced Chicago's growth throughout the 20th century and has inspired city planners worldwide.

Preceding page: *The Heald Square Monument, Lorado Taft's 1941 sculpture of George Washington with two financiers of the American Revolution, is dwarfed by Marina City.* This page, top to bottom: *Mainstay of mass transit, an "El" train rushes across the Chicago River. Washington, Morris, and Saloman in bronze stand in Heald Square. Parking space for Marina City residents winds upward through the lower 18 levels of each tower.*

Preceding page: *The Wrigley Building is a landmark on the lakefront skyline. Its bold clock tower and rich ornaments embody 1920's confidence. This page, clockwise: The Wrigley Building's design was inspired by a Renaissance tower in Seville, Spain. White terra-cotta worked in ornate patterns conceals its steel underpinnings. The camera angle tilts the Wrigley Building toward the neighboring Tribune Tower.*

This page, clockwise: *In the Tribune Plaza, a statue of Revolutionary patriot Nathan Hale honors Army Reservists. The Tribune Tower's medieval-style detailing includes flying buttresses around its apex. Henry Hering's bas-relief sculpture,* Defense, *on the Michigan Avenue Bridge recalls the 1812 Fort Dearborn massacre near the site of today's downtown. Opposite: Gothic Revival meets skyscraper in the Tribune Tower, built from the prize-winning design in a competition organized in 1922 by the newspaper the building houses.*

Chicago also anticipated developments elsewhere and paid great respect to the making of money and to those who made it. Great Chicago names have generally been the names of great merchants: Sears, Montgomery Ward, Marshall Field. The city that came into being entirely because its location was the best possible meeting point for buyers and sellers is frankly proud of its commercial life and of its heritage of trend-setting architecture commissioned by merchants and industrialists. The Loop's Heald Square Monument provides an example of the predominant values of Chicagoans, or at least of those who commission works of art. George Washington appears not with soldiers or with framers of the Constitution, but with Robert Morris and Haym Salomon, financiers who lent the fledgling nation money to wage its war of independence.

Yet Chicago's citizens, for the most part, have been workers rather than capitalists. From the time when plows first cut the prairies, Chicago's importance as a transport center made the city a way station for immigrants en route to new lives. The Germans and Irish who came to dig the canals were first: Swedes followed, and then Poles and other eastern Europeans. Among these hopeful, ambitious men and women were many who stayed to work in factories or in the Union Stock Yards, a collection point for livestock that opened just south of the city limits in 1865. Eventually it became the nation's most important cattle-trade center and a major employer of the new emigrants.

By 1910, half the city's population was foreign-born. During World War I, African-

Preceding page: *By night, the floodlit Wrigley Building, with the neighboring Chicago River as a reflecting pool, becomes a glamorous Michigan Avenue icon.* This page, clockwise: *The sliced-off top of Associates Center makes a skyline diamond. The 42-story Prudential Building (1955) was the first major Chicago structure to be built after World War II. North Michigan Avenue tenants get a clear view of Grant Park.* Opposite: *Strong 20th-century forms face Michigan Avenue.*

Preceding pages, left: *British sculptor Henry Moore's* Large Interior Form *(1982) stands in the Art Institute's North Garden.* Right: *One of animal sculptor Edward Kemeys' pair of ten-foot-long bronze lions commands a Michigan Avenue streetscape.* Opposite, clockwise: *Treasures of the Art Institute's collections include Grant Wood's* American Gothic, *perhaps the most famous American painting, Andy Warhol's* Mao, *and Georges Seurat's* Sunday Afternoon on the Isle of La Grande Jatte. *This page: Banners, flowers, and lions on sentry duty make a carnival of the Art Institute steps. Carl Milles'* Triton Fountain *(below), an adaptation of one at the sculptor's home on a Swedish island, is the centerpiece of a popular summer restaurant at the museum.*

Americans from the South seeking economic opportunity poured into Chicago, just as the Europeans before them had come. Chicago became a place known for its neighborhoods, each with its own ethnic character. Neighborhoods were continually evolving as the groups which arrived first moved outward toward larger houses and greener open space, a process that quickened as the tracks of the "El," Chicago's system of elevated trains, extended out to the city limits and beyond. For instance, the area around the stockyards and the huge meat-processing plants of "Packingtown" was first home to immigrants from Ireland and Germany, later to Swedes, and later still to Poles and Lithuanians. Chicago's strong tradition of ethnic enclaves produced, on the positive side, areas with real community spirit, each with a distinctive national character. On the negative side, complete segregation all too often resulted. Chicago's greatest stand against this destructive trend took place during the 1950's in Hyde Park, the neighborhood surrounding the University of Chicago. Hyde Park community members pulled together, planned effective redevelopment, and emerged a proudly multiracial professional community.

This page, top to bottom: *The Chicago Public Library Cultural Center (1897) is given an airy quality by its glass domes. A mosaic wall with characters in ancient languages by Louis Comfort Tiffany enriches the marble interior of the Center which is the site of frequent arts performances. Pigeons caught by a fast shutter hang in midair before the Center's limestone facade.*
Opposite: *Designed after a fountain at Versailles but twice the size of the model, the 1927 Buckingham Memorial Fountain in Grant Park sends 133 jets of water skyward.*

*Artfully illuminated each evening from May to September, Buckingham Fountain seems to glow from within as patterns of color play on the moving water.*

This page, clockwise: *Spanish-born Joan Miró's* Chicago *greets the public with open arms.* Chicago Picasso *faces the Miró sculpture across Washington Street. Alexander Calder's* Flamingo *stretches over nearby Federal Plaza.* Opposite: *38 floors of offices above a four-story television and radio studio make up the riverfront NBC Tower at Cityfront Center (1989) on Illinois Street.*

"Late last night, when we
were all in bed,
Old lady Leary left a lantern
in her shed.
When the cow kicked it over,
she winked her eye and
said,
'There'll be a hot time in the
old town tonight.'
Fire! Fire! Fire!"

Generations of folklorists
have laid the blame for the
Chicago Fire of 1871 on Mrs.
O'Leary's cow. While the great
conflagration did indeed start in
an Irish neighborhood in what
was then the southwestern part
of the city, its actual origin has
never been established. The
results of the blaze were far from
uncertain, however. Driven by
brisk winds, the fire raced north
and east toward the lake, destroy-
ing four square miles of property
in a long band parallel to the
lake shore that stretched as far
north as today's Lincoln Park.
The city lost 300 inhabitants,
over 17,000 houses, and one-
third of its wealth. But not even
a calamity on such a grand scale
could stop the action in this
bustling place. In fact, busi-
nesses grasped the opportunity
to update their buildings using
new technologies which were to
transform the shape of Chicago
and of cities generally: the
elevator and the steel skeleton
frame.

This page, top to bottom: *The arch
from Adler and Sullivan's Stock
Exchange Building (1893) which was
razed in 1972, now graces an Art
Institute garden. Orchestra Hall is the
home of the world famous Chicago
Symphony Orchestra. Traders buy
and sell frozen pork bellies with
shouts, hand signals, and high
technology at the Chicago Mercantile
Exchange.* Opposite: *Symbol of a city,
the Chicago Theater's huge sign juts
with a jazzy impudence from the 1921
movie palace's terra-cotta facade.*

Among the greatest of Chicago's distinctions is its acknowledged position as the birthplace of modern urban architecture. The ambitious young architects who flocked to Chicago in the post-fire years used engineering advances to create a form quite new in the world—the very tall building that the steel frame made possible. Eager to put their stamp on the downtown springing up from the ashes, they turned the Loop into a proving ground for the new large-scale buildings. Among these young people was the engineer William Le Baron Jenney, who designed the eleven-story Home Insurance Building. The world's first skyscraper, it was supported not by its walls but by a skeleton made of steel beams. It would appear modest indeed among the gleaming towers of the Loop today had it not been torn down in the 1930's. The technique was an immediate success, widely imitated from the first. Not only could steel-frame buildings rise to unprecedented heights, but they also allowed large amounts of wall space to be given over to windows, thus bringing light into the building interior, and they could be expanded upward or outward as necessary. And, in a once-burned city that was twice shy, they offered the great attraction of being fire resistant.

Louis Sullivan, a young architect from Boston, was quick to incorporate Jenney's technological breakthrough into his own philosophy of architecture.

*An "El" train roars through a skyscraper "canyon" above Lake Street, the northern boundary of the Loop, where ever-higher towers have risen at the city's valuable commercial core.*

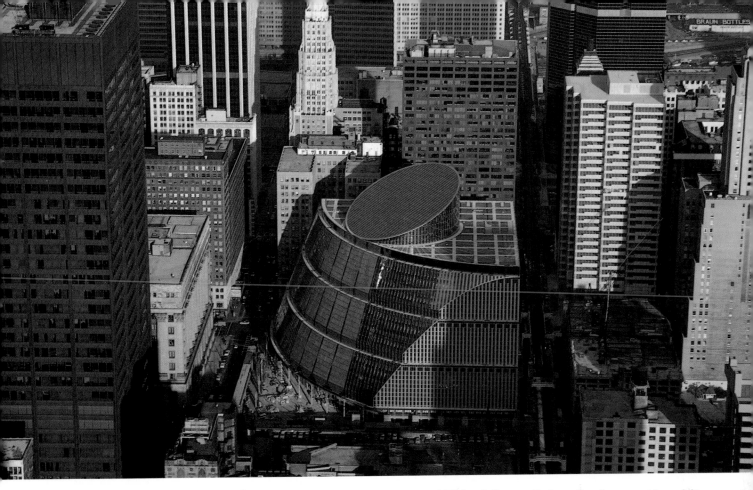

Preceding page, above: "El" tracks take a dramatic right-angle turn at Lake and Wabash Streets. Below: Intricate cast-iron foliage wreathes the ground-floor windows of Louis Sullivan's Carson Pirie Scott department store. Banners wave near the landmark clock at Marshall Field and Company on State Street, one of the nation's first great department stores. This page, above: A curved, inward-sloping glass facade topped by a glass cylinder defines the State of Illinois Center, the hub of state government. Below: A commercial neighborhood contrasts with the high-rises of the Loop.

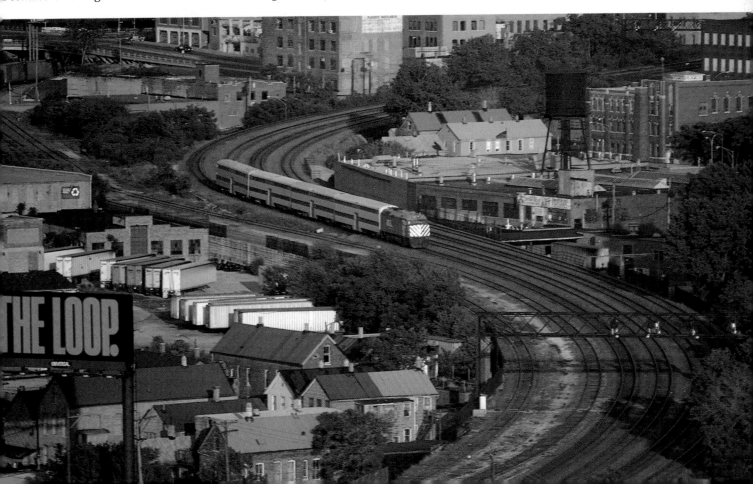

Monument á la Bête Debout, *a 30-foot-high Jean Dubuffet sculpture of white fiberglass edged in black, stands in the plaza of the State of Illinois Center.*

"Form ever follows function," Sullivan wrote, but the idea was a strange one in turn-of-the-century America, where eastern designers modeled their work on European Renaissance buildings or, more commonly, on later adaptations of Renaissance styles. Sullivan's structures combined simplified forms with brilliant ornamentation designed expressly for each building. Surviving examples include the arch from Sullivan's and his partner Dankmar Adler's Chicago Stock Exchange building and the wrought-iron decoration on the architect's last major commission, the Carson Pirie Scott department store. The uncluttered lines of Sullivan's buildings and those of his contemporaries influenced not only the look of downtown Chicago but contemporary urban building design worldwide.

A young man named Frank Lloyd Wright worked in Sullivan and Adler's offices for a short time in the 1880's. When the senior partners found out that he was working on his own projects on company time, they fired him. Wright started his own office in suburban Oak Park and became one of the greatest architects (certainly the most influential in the realm of domestic building) America has ever produced. The sweeping eaves and horizontal flow of Wright's "Prairie Houses" expressed kinship with the land and served to integrate the houses into the landscape. More than two dozen Wright houses stand today in Oak Park, including Wright's own home and studio, which visitors may tour.

*Light spills through the rooftop cylinder of the State of Illinois Center into a great central atrium (top). A rich abstract design of sun and shadow fills the cylinder (below).*

Biograph Theater on North Lincoln Avenue is where bank robber John Dillinger, Public Enemy #1, was gunned down by federal agents in July, 1934. Below: At the First National Bank Plaza, a 70-foot-long Chagall mosaic wall, The Four Seasons, captures images of Chicago in fragments of stone and glass.

Hyde Park's Robie House on the University of Chicago campus, the most famous of all the Prairie Houses, is also open to visitors.

After World War I, building styles grew more elaborate. High-rises with European-style decorations concealing their steel-frame structures rose throughout the Loop and north of it along Michigan Avenue. The Wrigley Building and the Gothic Revival Tribune Tower are the best known. The Depression brought these fanciful times to an abrupt end, and few significant downtown buildings appeared until after World War II. By then, a famous European architect, Bauhaus director Ludwig Mies van der Rohe, had fled the Nazis and become head of the architecture school at the Illinois Institute of Technology. Mies van der Rohe's buildings and those he inspired drew attention to the forms beneath the surfaces of buildings even more than Sullivan's creations had. Starting with the boxlike Prudential Tower in 1955, a new generation of notable buildings has risen. The Sears Tower of 1974 is the tallest in the world, but in the years since its completion dozens of distinctive shapes have been added to the Chicago skyline: the Associates Center's prominent angled diamond of a top, and the intriguing outward curve of 333 West Wacker. Chicago, modern architecture's home town, remains one of its greatest showplaces.

This page, top to bottom: *Sea lions swim in their pool at the Lincoln Park Zoo, home to more than 2,200 animal species. Formal flowerbeds surround Lincoln Park Conservatory, where four glass houses built in the 1890's cover three acres. Autumn sunlight dapples the University of Chicago campus in Hyde Park.*

Preceding page: *This 15-foot bronze statue of the great Swedish botanist Carolus Linnaeus stands on the University of Chicago's Midway Plaisance. This page: Frank Lloyd Wright designed this residence in the historic district of suburban Oak Park. Below: The 909 Robie House in Hyde Park is the best-known of Wright's "Prairie Houses." Overleaf: The University of Chicago's Rockefeller Memorial Chapel honors the man whose money founded the institution in 1891.*

Above: *The National League's Chicago Cubs, longtime holdouts for old-fashioned afternoon games, gave in and illuminated Wrigley Field on August 8, 1988.* Below: *Comiskey Park is home turf for the city's American League team, the White Sox.* Opposite: *Lincoln Park, where winding, tree-lined paths frame lagoons and ponds, stretches along the lake shore just above the North Michigan Avenue shopping and business district.*

The same prosperous business people whose money sent Loop buildings skyward got the city's cultural institutions under way. Founded first was the Art Institute, which came into being in 1879, less than a decade after the fire. Dozens of wealthy boosters of the rebuilding city donated the art they owned to form the core of a collection that has become one of the country's finest, and includes many French Impressionist and Post-Impressionist paintings, and 20th-century American works like Edward Hopper's *Nighthawks*. Renovation in the 1970's re-inforced the art museum's ties to the commercial life of the city. The main trading room of the Chicago Stock Exchange, de-signed by Adler and Sullivan and demolished in 1972, was recon-structed within the Institute's new wing, and a water garden was created on the Institute grounds around the Stock Exchange's graceful entry arch.

Architectural distinction and fine museums were important, but the ambitious young city needed a prestigious university even more. In 1892, the lack was remedied and the University of Chicago sprang up almost over-night in what was then the southern suburb of Hyde Park. Money to fund it came not from a group of business leaders, but from a single individual: John D. Rockefeller, the millionaire at the helm of Standard Oil. Rockefeller's startup grant made it possible to attract renowned scholars by offering far higher salaries than any other univer-sity was paying at the time. Nine college presidents were on the

*The Chicago Bears play football at Soldier Field, constructed in 1922 as a war memorial. Doric columns rise 100 feet above its bleachers.*

first faculty roster. Rockefeller also paid for a coherent plan for future architectural development that is largely responsible for the attractive, well-ordered appearance of the campus today. The original design and buildings by architect Henry Ives Cobb adopted a late Gothic style reminiscent of the medieval English universities. While buildings added since World War II often vary in design, their architects have taken into consideration compatibility with Cobb's Gothic Revival structures.

Designing modern college buildings that will fit in on a Gothic Revival campus is a typically Chicagoan challenge, one of the kind that the city's builders have proved adept at meeting. Chicago has always been a juncture of opposites, the place where great prairies meet the Great Lakes, where highrises soar to improbable heights above vast, flat expanses of land and water. Today's Chicago is hardly without problems, many of which it shares with other large cities. But those who have the Chicago spirit are confident. The city which invented skyscrapers, mail order catalogues, and modern urban planning surely has more ingenious solutions to come.

*The simple, granite Adler Planetarium, completed in 1930, was the first in the U.S.* Below: *Nearby on Northerly Island is the Thaddeus Kosciuszko Memorial, a tribute from Chicago's Polish-American community to the man who engineered important fortifications during the American Revolution.*

This page: *The Field Museum of Natural History in Grant Park houses 16 million objects including dinosaur bones, mummies, and collections of Native American and Pacific Islander art. It is the world's largest Georgia marble building.*

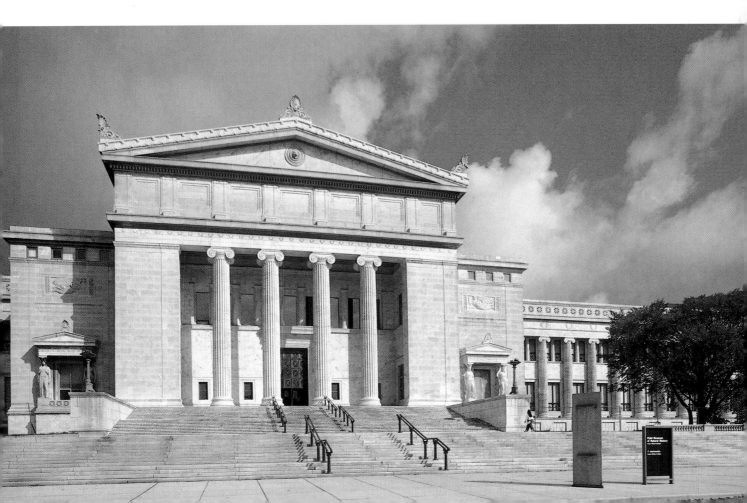

Above: *The Water Tower, one of only a handful of Chicago buildings spared by the Great Fire of 1871, stands amid strapping young neighbors.* Below: *This shot makes close companions of the 1869 Water Tower and the 100-story John Hancock Tower.* Opposite: *The late-day interaction of light and shadow brings out the Gothic detailing of the Water Tower's Joliet limestone.* Following pages: *White lights in the trees give North Michigan Avenue a holiday sparkle. Glass-enclosed elevators offer shoppers breathtaking ascents and descents at the center of Water Tower Place, a seven-level shopping complex.*

# Index of Photography

All photographs are courtesy of The Image Bank,
except where indicated (*).

| Page Number | Photographer | Page Number | Photographer |
|---|---|---|---|
| Title Page | Wolfgang Kaehler* | 32 Bottom | Santi Visalli |
| 3 | Andy Caulfield | 33 | Nicholas Foster |
| 4-5 | Eddie Hironaka | 34 | Jake Rajs |
| 6 | Eddie Hironaka | 35 | Marc Romanelli |
| 7 Top | Patti McConville | 36 Top Left | David W. Hamilton |
| 7 Center | Eddie Hironaka | 36 Top Right | Paul Slaughter |
| 7 Bottom | Gregory Heisler | 36 Bottom | Marvin E. Newman |
| 8 | David W. Hamilton | 37 | David J. Maenza |
| 9 | David J. Maenza | 38 Top | Cliff Feulner |
| 10 | David W. Hamilton | 38 Center | David J. Maenza |
| 11 | Patti McConville | 38 Bottom | David W. Hamilton |
| 12 Top | David W. Hamilton | 39 | Nick Nicholson |
| 12 Bottom | Andy Caulfield | 40-41 | Patti McConville |
| 13 | Michael Melford | 42 Top | Giuliano Colliva |
| 14-15 | David J. Maenza | 42 Bottom Left | Jim Green* |
| 16 | Giuliano Colliva | 42 Bottom Right | Patti McConville |
| 17 | Andy Caulfield | 43 (2) | David J. Maenza |
| 18 | David W. Hamilton | 44 | David W. Hamilton |
| 19 Top | Marvin E. Newman | 45 Top | Marc Romanelli |
| 19 Center | David J. Maenza | 45 Bottom | David J. Maenza |
| 19 Bottom | Marc Romanelli | 46 Top | Andy Caulfield |
| 20 | Giuliano Colliva | 46 Bottom | David J. Maenza |
| 21 Top Left | Andrea Pistolesi | 47 Top & Center | David J. Maenza |
| 21 Top Right | Tim Bieber | 47 Bottom | Santi Visalli |
| 21 Bottom | Marc Romanelli | 48 | Andrea Pistolesi |
| 22 Top Left | Marvin E. Newman | 49 Top | Patti McConville |
| 22 Top Right | David J. Maenza | 49 Bottom | Jim Green* |
| 22 Bottom | Walter Bibikow | 50-51 | Andrea Pistolesi |
| 23 | Andrea Pistolesi | 52 (2) | David J. Maenza |
| 24-25 | Eddie Hironaka | 53 | David J. Maenza |
| 26 Top Left | Marc Romanelli | 54-55 | Tim Bieber |
| 26 Top Right | Frank A. Cezus/Stockphotos, Inc.* | 56 Top | Giuliano Colliva |
| 26 Bottom | David J. Maenza | 56 Bottom | Andy Caulfield |
| 27 | Patti McConville | 57 Top | David J. Maenza |
| 28 | John Lewis Stage | 57 Bottom | Andrea Pistolesi |
| 29 | Andrea Pistolesi | 58 Top | Eddie Hironaka |
| 30 Top Left | Gregory Heisler | 58 Bottom | David W. Hamilton |
| 30 Top Right | Santi Visalli | 59 | Andrea Pistolesi |
| 30 Bottom | Marvin E. Newman | 60 | David J. Maenza |
| 31 (2) | Marvin E. Newman | 61 | Marvin E. Newman |
| 32 Top & Center | Jim Green* | 62-63 | Andy Caulfield |

Preceding pages: *A city's proud name is spelled out on the Chicago Theater's marquee.*